A Cloud Where the Birds Rise

A BOOK ABOUT LOVE AND BELONGING

Author and playwright, Michael Harding writes a regular column for The Irish Times. He is the author of several novels as well as award-winning, bestselling memoirs including Staring at Lakes (Winner of the Bord Gáis Energy Book of the Year), Hanging with the Elephant, Talking to Strangers, On Tuesdays I'm a Buddhist, Chest Pain and What is Beautiful in the Sky. He also has a regular podcast with reflections on life on Patreon.

Jacob Stack is from Donegal, Ireland. He studied Fine Art Printmaking in Limerick School of Art and Design, graduating in 2012. Jacob has exhibited work in solo and group shows nationally and internationally in London, New York, and L.A. He was shortlisted in the AOI World Illustration Awards 2017.

A Cloud Where the Birds Rise

A BOOK ABOUT LOVE AND BELONGING

MICHAEL HARDING

Illustrations by
JACOB STACK

HACHETTE
BOOKS
IRELAND

The Venerable Panchen Otrul Rinpoche,
Jampa Ling, Bawnboy (MH)

For Mam and Da; the family;
and in memory of Louisa (JS)

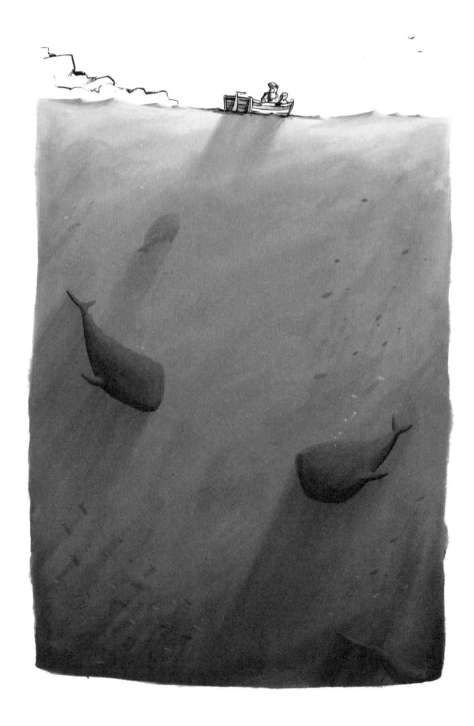

Contents

Introduction

I encounter strangers everywhere: at filling stations, Gala shops and in small coffee docks from Mullingar to Warsaw. I listen to them carefully and recycle their stories because I am constantly amazed at their wisdom. And it's not difficult to deduce that, for most people, love is a mixture of joy and sorrow. One day recently I noticed a woman on the street struggling for breath. She was so fragile that her daughter gripped her arm to prevent her falling. I realised I knew her.

'I didn't recognise you with the mask,' I exclaimed. And we spoke about her health.

'Well,' she said after a little reflection, 'there's some nights I sleep and there's some nights I don't sleep.'

It reminded me of another woman I met long ago in Mullingar. She stood behind me in the post office and shared her troubles as we queued. A man was supposed to install cable television for her that morning but never arrived. And her husband was still in bed even though it was noon.

'Do you know what I'm going to tell you,' she said, drawing breath, preparing herself to deliver the truth.

'If it's not one thing, it's another.'

She was referencing the patience that life requires. Sometimes we're up and sometimes we're down. There's nothing can be done but to endure the good and the bad with equanimity. And there isn't a philosopher on earth that could add much more than footnotes to that insight.

I've been living in the hills above Lough Allen for years and I often say I live in County Leitrim which is not entirely true. The mountains and lake spread out before me are certainly in Leitrim but I'm actually standing in County Roscommon. The slopes of Arigna's coal-rich mountains nuzzle in behind me and shelter me from the Atlantic Sea storms. My home is a borderland and I love it. I have neighbours here. I belong here. I am part of a family here.

I also spend time travelling: wandering around hotels, arts centres, supermarkets and other public spaces from Cork to Donegal. I talk to strangers whose stories are always underwritten by love or the lack thereof. In fact, I never met anyone for whom something else was more important than love.

Lovers commit continual acts of self-abandonment. In the embrace of love, they reach beyond their personal boundaries; bliss achieved in self-forgetfulness.

'I am yours,' the lover says, 'and I give myself to you.'

But sometimes I don't want to give myself to anyone. I need to be alone. For sure I want to be hugged, loved and cherished but occasionally I want to snuggle into the little shell of my own self. So I head for the coast where the ocean affords me magnificent solitude. Where I can turn my back on modernity and allow the avatars and mentor deities of my imagination to walk with me on the strand.

The little shell of the self is rinsed clean by the waves. It's as if I'm not listening with my ears any longer and I experience a sense of belonging even deeper than with people.

I love meeting someone for coffee and lingering in their presence for half an hour, exploring the small catastrophes of ordinary life with them. But equally I love to walk along the shoreline, where the waves break, and the wind wraps itself around me and I feel like a bird soaring in the clouds and delightfully alone.

My soul is a borderland; a place where I am balanced between living on the outside and living on the inside; between the love that makes me human, and the ultimate solitude that is my destiny, and where all belonging is completed.

Perhaps the woman struggling for breath on the street knew the truth of it when she said that there's some nights she sleeps, and there's some nights she doesn't.

Tiny spaces in the Universe: thoughts on Love

When we long for impossible
things, our hearts open.
That's love.

If there was one thing that made
me feel alive, it was being in love.
That was my salvation.
That was the thing that made
everything else coherent.
Love made meaning of the world.
Everything belonged and was
bright when love sat at the centre.

The room is never empty.
   As long as love lacks surveillance.
As long as love is sung, spoken and
   danced, the house is never empty.
Because love is everywhere.
   Behind us. Above us. Below us.
Beside us. Inside and outside.
   Everywhere.

Once upon a time in an imaginary world, there lived two men in a single house on an island in a lough; two brothers who loved each other magnificently. Even as children, they had looked after each other. If one went fishing, the other would go along as well, just to keep an eye on him.

When they were young men, they had travelled to the mainland in search of women. But if one had an interest in a particular lady, the other would have just as equal a claim and, in the end, neither of them married. They remained on their island after their parents died, with a clean-scrubbed table and a fiddle hanging on the wall. And if the fiddle ever came down off the wall, the other would open a drawer and take out a flute and join in. People said they could play tunes like birds, in unison like the flight of geese. They were one at all times, the harmony between them was beyond human intelligence.

Except for apples. One of them loved apples. The other couldn't keep an apple down.

One night, the apple lover was at home and the other fellow was on the mainland. It was winter and there was ice on the lough. In a deep sleep, the apple lover heard a voice. He woke. He could still hear it. In the frosty air, it travelled from the middle of the lake, from where his brother, the one who couldn't keep an apple down, was caught far out on the ice.

He couldn't row to shore. He couldn't walk on the cold ice. So, he called his brother. And his brother heard him. And his brother answered his call.

The apple lover pulled out a boat from under the willows at the lough shore and pushed it out onto the ice. He took a pitchfork to break the frozen water. Made it deep into the white lough. Deep, but not deep enough. He followed the faint cries of his brother, the boy who could never keep an apple down.

In the morning, their boats were seen from the mainland, out in the middle of the lough. The two men had frozen to death — the boats were so close together, their prows were touching.

Then, a flight was called at Knock Airport. The gates opened and I saw the little chink that sometimes opens in the universe and enables love to manifest in human form.

And it happened again and again, each time a flight was called. And it happened at each table, between each couple and in every family cluster.

That strange birth of pain and love that comes unexpectedly to the human heart as a single event when a family is being rent asunder. It's called 'saying goodbye'.

This is what the long miles were about, I thought. The awkward silences, the small chats over breakfasts that no one wanted and the pretence at reading newspapers. This is what it was all for. This was the thing that no one wanted to miss. The thing that everyone wanted to get right. To say goodbye, and to say it well in gesture and word.

Gradually, I saw that it was happening all around me all the time in a thousand hidden moments. The farewells happened with such discretion that they were hardly noticeable. Sometimes, no more than a whisper in the ear. The last touch of a hand at the departure gates. A little tugging on a coat sleeve. This wasn't a single dramatic apparition of God, but a hundred tiny nativities of love shimmering in damp eyes and opening arms. The lips moving so clearly that I could spell the words: 'Don't forget the sausages', 'Say hello to everyone', 'Happy New Year'.

The last moment of physical intimacy is always a miracle.

To breathe in love for a second and then hold it for another year, as if each year was an eternity.

When I met the love of my life,
     my sadness dissolved.
I felt like a boy inside, madly in love
     but with no words to articulate it.
Until she came closer and touched my arm
and, for a moment, I was released
     from the burden of being me.

You meet someone whose path in life has been identical. And you don't have to say what you're thinking because they know what you're thinking. And you know them more intimately than your own soul.

'I thought you were gone,' her mother said, full of sudden hope.

'I just came back for this,' the daughter replied, reaching for the blue cardigan, and in that moment her mother spoke her name and gave her a final hug.

There is a hug that happens after all the hugs, which is more valuable than gold. It is the extra hug. It is the hug that happens when someone is leaving, when the goodbyes have been said, and the fussing over luggage has been done twice over, and when the tears have been avoided and the manly, coherent hugs have all been delivered and the emigrant is about to step away and become a ghost. And then something is remembered. The keys. A passport. Or a cardigan. And, at that last moment, the one who is about to leave turns again and says, 'I forgot something,' and suddenly there is time for one last, enormous hug; that extra hug that a child can carry with them across the mountains and over the ocean.

We stayed awake wondering who we were —
where we were coming from and what
we were doing and what was happening to us.
Because something was happening to us.
We were opening a tiny space in the universe
where a couple can escape the loneliness
that each individual is condemned to.
Just for a few hours, we were in a space
called 'us'. And it was wonderful.

But, even then, it was clear to me
   that love was the most important
thing in the world, and that, eventually,
      I must fall in love with someone
who would never disappear.

Since I was a teenager,
   I have always been in love.
There's always someone, a person,
   a cat or ghost touches me.
      Because love is a capacity.

The entire world was described
by ancient mystics as a kiss.
It was where the invisible world
touched this world. A kiss was
nothing in itself. It was what
two people did, and it was
how they connected.

I didn't feel shame with her.
   And maybe that is where love begins.
When someone can take away the
   shame and let you be who you are.

Through each new day, the lines
that define one individual as different
from another were dissolving.
There was no way to use the word '/'
anymore. '/' didn't function or make
sense. '/' was not human.
There was only 'us'.

I always hoped I'd fall in love.
And that if I grew up and fell
in love, life would be easy.
That's what I thought.
But I grew up in Ireland, and
it sometimes seems that Irish people
have no hope. We live in despair.
For women, the great disappointment
is men — for men,
it's practically everything.

Our home was a paradise of
small things that we could rely on.
The open fire. The bottle of wine.
The snow at Christmas. The eyes
of a child. The company of friends.
The regularity of the farmer next
door completing his chores
season after season.

When we first fell in love,
we used language to measure each other.
To name each other. Asking questions
about what our separate lives had been
like before we met. We were trying
to explain each self to the other.

In her presence, I have meaning,
even if it is only to make sure
        the coal buckets are full.
Alone, without her for even a day,
   I can barely survive. I am devastated
        as I eat my porridge in solitude
and silence, and place a single bowl
in the dishwasher with my single spoon.

'I will weave my solitude around yours,'
I whispered at her sleeping figure,
'until we are both grey-haired and
silent in our separate armchairs,
with no more need to speak.'

The Collective Hug: thoughts on Dying

In rural Ireland, that's life; funerals are part and parcel of every ordinary day.
There are graveyards in Leitrim, Mayo and Roscommon – on the edges of every small town in Ireland – that open wide the earth for such weekly tragedies, where people cling to each other in the face of death's conundrum.

Burying the dead is not a private act
  in rural Ireland. It's like a collective hug.
It's a ritual during which physical closeness
  is fundamental to the communal expression
of grief. An entire parish squeezed into
    some little church and gathered around
the broken mourners, draped in black
    clothes, as they sit frozen and
        bewildered in the front pews.

There is a strange longing in
human beings to suffer wakefully
    with others rather than sleep alone.

As humans we need each other.
    And we need each other's pain to
waken us. To acknowledge that there
    is nothing but this moment,
        this exquisite here and now.

Letting go of life might
    be as natural as letting go
of a single breath.
    The end of the tune.

The truth is that it's not easy to die, but in
    the cloud of coronavirus it was unbearable.
Knowing that all the stories and love songs
      of a lifetime will be taken in a body
bag to the graveyard without the full pomp
of a warm, Irish funeral. A lonely coffin
before the altar, without ritual or ceremony
      apart from perhaps a single minister with
a pot of holy water. No throng of mourners
crushing towards the front pews to shake
      the family's hands and no heaving in the
graveyard under a hundred umbrellas. Not
      even rain in the dry months, that might
fall on a coffin like tender kisses from
heaven itself as the remains are
      folded back into the earth.

Sometimes, we live through
moments of intensity – like a death –
and it's so overwhelming that we
replay the moment over and over
again. And then, one day,
the event arises as usual,
but it's different. We see it in a
new light. There is no reason
for this. It just happens.

We lived in an unchanging world
in Leitrim and we watched him through
the seasons moving cattle or mowing
meadows or lodging bales of silage into
   the rusting red shed to the south of
our land. We sat on the porch listening to
the sound of the tractor in the distance.
   When he died, a shadow drifted across
the garden that would not go away.

And after he died, I could still sense
     his presence in the shadows around
the galvanised shed or in the meadow
beyond our trees. The hay barn to the south
     of our land stood silent, but for the
wind in the rusty sheets. Roxie our cat
would still go down there and sit in the
     hay that he had saved the previous year.
When I went near the shed, Roxie would
come out and rub her back against my leg,
     pleading with me for attention, as if she
were asking something.
     Where is he?

It lashed rain in the churchyard
   and the oak coffin was splattered
so fiercely that one devout lady
   whispered in my ear that she
felt the Mother of God was in the
vicinity, weeping for her own child.
Such is the lyrical imagination
   of country folk.

Life is passing. It is over in a flash, and the only place to find the kingdom of heaven is in the present moment. And there are no teachings in any tradition worth so much as an aspirin.

Every tune comes out of silence.
But sometimes there is only silence.
Like a full stop.

I kissed her forehead before
        the coffin lid was closed
down on her. The last kiss,
I told myself, must last my lifetime.

Now that my mother was buried,
  there was no meaning in the house.
Her clothes didn't mean anything
      and the ornaments and objects
she had gathered, hoarded and
   loved for fifty years, that she had
crammed onto every mantelpiece and
into every china cabinet in the house,
      were suddenly bereft of any
further significance.

I didn't say anything because
there is a grief that words
cannot soften and a pain
that no story can cure.

The afterlife to the Cavan man
was a big sleep, a great snooze,
    a long doze till Christ returned on
tiptoe at the dawn of a new tomorrow.
    The grave was just another bed,
and eternity was a silence undisturbed.

I can't let go of the consolation
that fading into the universe at death
might be natural and that death
may hold the greatest possibility of all.

After a gig in Cork, I went to my hotel and ordered a drink and brought it to the residents' lounge. I was sitting on a big sofa when a woman came over to me.

'I hope you don't mind me sitting here,' she said, as she sat beside me.

'I read something that you wrote in the newspaper about your mother being a widow,' she said. 'Actually, I'm a widow too,' she added. 'I'm fine most of the time, but I dread Christmas.'

'What was your husband's name?' I wondered.

She spoke it, and I felt his presence well up inside her as she began to weep.

I couldn't get her out of my mind, even during Christmas, so I tried writing to her for the New Year, the kind of letter that I would never have been able to write to my own mother when her husband had died:

I was thinking of you over the Christmas, of the years that stretch before you now as a widow. And I was thinking of all the years you spent with your beloved and all the drama at the end of his life. How familiar you were with his body, with all its curves and edges and the smell of the sheets. And now all you have left is the emptiness in the bedroom when you walk into it, going from room to room, as if walking from one empty shell to another.

Believe me when I say that the house where my mother had lived became a shell too, where she tried to protect herself from loneliness after her husband died. But please don't protect yourself like that. Embrace the memories that you shared with me. The way he left things in the bathroom when he had finished washing, the sight of his clothes on the floor, the texture of his damp discarded towel. Don't hide from the terror of that absence. Don't be afraid to wonder how it might have been if you had grown old together. And when the grief has fully surfaced, make a mug of tea in the kitchen. Don't be afraid of that ritual you always did with him, that collaboration of boiling a kettle or laughing through the soap operas.

And go for a walk in the garden. Examine the dead plants and the frosty clay that was so full of flower last

July. Consider the resilience of cherry trees, the tight lawn's endurance and the understated dignity of the sharp hedge lines that he trimmed for decades.

Walk along the avenue where, in funereal solemnity, he made his final journey away from you, out the gate on his sons' shoulders before they put his coffin in the hearse. You always worried about him leaving you, but you never thought he'd leave like that.

Walk back up the avenue and plan your future.

The flowerbeds will still need attention in January. Promise yourself to begin again. He is gone now. Last year will be on his gravestone and this is another year. Commit to it and to now — even if now is empty. And when the flowers are stale on his grave, bring new ones. Say they are for him, and leave them there and then walk away. Which is only what any of us try to do after a funeral, with the help of others.

I walked outside and found her. She happened to be sitting again looking at Sliabh an Iarainn across the lake. I joined her at a wrought-iron table on the new patio.

We were looking at the mountain in the distance, beyond the wide waters of Lough Allen. To our side were the oaks and beeches, the willows and alders puffed out with luminous green leaves.

Although in the sloping fields around us there were no cattle, no black beasts with warm furry heads reaching their snouts across the fence to be touched by a human hand. Because our neighbour's hand would touch no more, and his feet would move no more across the fields. He was at rest in the cemetery on the far side of Arigna Valley. If the beloved was thinking about him at that moment, she did not say. Nor did I speak. Because there is a time for everything. A time for stories. And a time for silence.

Bric-a-Brac and Peaked Hats: thoughts on Ageing

For a man of my years, the sight of young people wandering about can be an unsettling experience. I began humming 'Forever Young' by Bob Dylan as I checked in at the hotel desk. I took off my glasses because I don't think I look very cool with glasses – and I was trying desperately to be cool, amid the throng of youths. The receptionist was confused because I had filled in my name on the wrong line.

'Please,' she said, 'put your name here, on this line.' She pointed to the correct spot.

I said, 'I'm sorry, I don't have my glasses with me.' She looked at me and said,

'They're on your head'.

When my daughter left, myself and
the beloved were in the kitchen,
      looking at the empty nest for
the first time. She was gone.
And we were alone. You can feel it, right?
The silence of the little kitchen.

My eye tried to avoid the mess on
every shelf, the private letters strewn on
the floor and jam jars with old biros
and fountain pens as dead as doornails.
My narrative. My life. My fountain pens.
My manuscripts and ledgers and books.
But none of it retained meaning.
It was all the bric-a-brac of a bygone life.

People over fifty just don't sleep that well. They wake suddenly, as if staring into an abyss.

Maybe I've always attracted old people's attention. Or maybe it's because I always knew that the older a person is, the more stories they have. Or maybe it's because I was always afraid of ageing and couldn't admit it to myself.

Old people don't need the sea to feel powerless. Fragility grows with the years and something unnameable roars at me, even in the fury of rush-hour traffic, like an ocean that must be faced eventually.

And so, we walked. Uneasy.
   I suppose like many couples with
grey hair and creaking bones and
   malfunctioning organs. We walked
in silence because we had too much
   to say without knowing how.

I asked the cardiologist at the end of
    my final check-up how exactly did
I get a heart attack. After all is said
    and done, I exercised and I wasn't
terribly overweight and I didn't drink
    to wild excesses. 'We all grow old,'
he said and smiled. 'And is there
anything in particular I should do?'
    I asked. 'Yes,' he replied.
'Enjoy life. It's later than you think.'

When I was young, I often sneered
at men who took refuge in gardens.
Until I found myself in the shimmering
leaves of the beech trees, seeking shelter,
and wondering if it was possible that
I had arrived at that moment of wisdom
when a man lifts his hands from the
plough, turns his back on the world
and finds peace in the garden.

On the threshold of old age,
when a man sees himself withering for
the first time, he panics. He needs his
partner's hand in ways he never did
before. He says 'hold me' too often,
until it sounds selfish.

The fact was that my peaked cap had begun to stick to my head. It happens to a man when he turns sixty-five — a mysterious glue of psychic attachment prevents the cap from coming off, even when he is eating his dinner. Some men are stuck to their caps for so long that if they took them off nobody would recognise them.

If there is one thing that proves
   that a man's perception of the world
is entirely deluded, it is his ability to
   hold an image of himself as heroic
   while his body deteriorates.

The betrayal of old age is more about turning in on oneself, rather than reaching out.

The older I get, the more silence
        envelops me. The past drifts farther
away and is of less importance.
        Even the quicksteps and jives of my
youth appear more distant as I age.

Old age is a time for hobbies.
People need to fill the days with something.
Take up water-colouring.
Do the things that they have
dreamed of doing for a lifetime.

Even an attic full of manuscripts that
I have sweated over down the years will
be lost. The clunky glass and brass
trophies and the awards I have won for
plays, books or performances that gather
dust on the shelves won't mean anything
in the passing of time.

Life slips by and we drift in directions that we never planned.

When we are young, life comes and goes like the ocean tide, and we get washed up in different places and can do nothing about it. But as we get older, something in the universe coheres. Friends and family grow around us with the elegance of differing branches on a tree. It's all random and we are powerless in it but, when in full bloom, the air feels like grace.

Talking About the Cat: thoughts on Marriage

I thought marriage might
protect me from depression.
Marriage is a happy thing.

I didn't want to spend all my life alone,
shovelling last night's ashes into a bucket
and staring into an empty fire grate
with only myself in the room.
I wanted company. I wanted someone
to cling to. Someone to love.

You see them sometimes in the supermarkets, tethered to the same trolley.

He's in a daze. He might see corn flakes on the shelf. He likes his corn flakes.

He reaches for the packet. She takes it from him and switches it for the muesli. And when his fingers touch the honey jar, she points to the organic one, and his fingers obey. 'That's better for you,' she says. And he doesn't disagree.

'What are you thinking?' she asked.
'Nothing,' I said, staring out the window.
Nothing I could actually tell you.
'I'm just looking at the donkeys.'

The cats were a good subject of conversation. It was light and cheerful. Not too complicated with emotion.

When we were together, we sat shoulder to shoulder on the sofa, and the remote control was like a wand that shielded me from intimacy. And when I went walking, I took my phone with me. It never rang, but I looked at it every few minutes, just in case.

'Don't forget milk on your way home.'
   It's one of the great gifts women have.
They can anticipate what you might
         need in a domestic situation.
   Of course I won't forget the milk,
he thinks. Does she suppose I'm stupid?
      Does she think I'm incapable of
   keeping the kitchen organised?

I suppose when young people start out,
they know as little about marriage as
they do about pension funds.

We all try to make love succeed.

Her hand touched my shoulder
    and I knew her immediately.
I turned around and there she was,
    radiant in the brilliant sunshine,
laughing and hugging me with
expressive enthusiasm that neither
    of us would have indulged in at
home in the Irish rain where only
    ambiguous emotions are valid.

'I was locked out of our hotel room and my wife, by sleeping so heavily, had betrayed me. I tied the pyjama top around my waist like a skirt and headed down the corridor in search of the lift. To my relief the reception area was empty. Distant voices of the night staff floated from the kitchen, where they were enjoying their midnight dinner. I sneaked in behind the reception desk, got the phone and dialled room 1003. Her voice was like salvation. Her voice was like the music of the heavens. How I love this woman, I thought. I need her so much. I depend on her.

'It's me,' I said. 'I locked myself out. Can you open the door?'

There was a long pause.

'Who's this?' she asked.

'It's me,' I said. 'It's fucking me.'

The most existential declaration of identity I had ever known.

'It's me,' I said. And it was. Me. Hiding under the reception desk of a Galway hotel.

But it was us, later, in the cosy bed. A couple. Married. Going forward.

You can never anticipate what will happen. You can only surf the future like a wave when it arrives and hold on to the promise that was made so public at the beginning: 'I will share this with you.'

Marriage is mysterious.
Impossible to understand. It is mystical,
   an ultimate truth that cannot be
apprehended by the intellect.
      In parts of Asia, it is called the
'great koan' – a riddle without a solution.
      For me, the beloved is the one
I walk with in the garden at night
      when we talk to the trees.

To avoid domestic, nuclear meltdown, it's sometimes good to take a break: from each other.

She's the one I needed. And not just when my heart failed. There were other times. It's mundane to say it, I know, but what makes a difference is not religion or faith at that critical moment, but the one who sits by your bedside.

One of the most common questions I'm asked is: What are you thinking? One of my most common answers I give is: Nothing.

In her wedding photographs,
   my mother smiles with abandon beneath
a flowery white hat, though she wears
   a cream suit rather than a bridal gown.
Her husband, a much older man,
   looks out from the same photographs
with uncertainty, as if he was wondering,
   Who got me into this?

I had nothing to report apart from the fact that it was raining or not raining, and that I had fed the cat or not fed the cat.

I remember walking on the beach at
Banna Strand many years ago with another
friend whose marriage had broken down.
We walked like old men, hauling ourselves
into the wind. The empty space
suited us as we staggered over the dunes.

'I don't know how your wife
puts up with you.' When he was gone,
I thought, neither do I.
But I suppose that's the mystery.

I want to hug and hold the beloved but,
sometimes, I don't because it seems
        too emotional a risk in public.
I am embarrassed to lash out all that
        feeling at an airport in front of so
many men in visor jackets and
        peaked caps. Though I have to admit
that arrival lounges are usually stuffed
        with men happily flinging their
                emotions in all directions.

'Ah, you're home,' I said quietly, gently,
as if she had just come back from a
neighbour's house and had not actually
been away for months.
I wanted to hug her, but I didn't.
I couldn't. I wanted to say,
'I have missed you,' but I didn't.

There is more to life than just holding hands, and the English dictionary offers a variety of similar verbs — to hold on, to hold up, to hold out and to hold forth. There is a way of being held, and of beholding, which is not just touching or being physical but a way of holding each other that makes us human.

Unbearable Beauty: thoughts on Nature

The first time I heard the sound of
a curlew, I thought it so forlorn that it
      sucked out all my neuroses and left
me as clean as an empty bowl.
Wilderness, I believed, was the mother of
all poetry. I loved it.

The field itself was full of yellow flowers.
I leaned on the gate and clung to the
serenity of it all for a moment and,
for that moment, the sun came out and
Leitrim appeared unbearably beautiful.

I stood long enough in the garden
to allow the blue of the sky and lake
to seep into my bones.

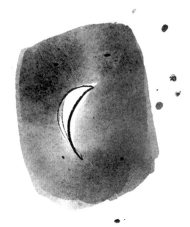

I once passed a winter on a wild headland
near Annagry in Donegal, just to
watch the ocean beat off the rocks
in the moonlight.

As I looked out from my hilltop cottage in the hills above Lough Allen, overlooking the mountains that stretch from the peaks of Cuilce to the slopes of Sliabh an Iarainn near Drumshanbo, I could assure myself that, for this time being, Leitrim was undoubtedly an auspicious place to live.

One morning, I looked out at tiny flecks of snow falling and at a coy blackbird sitting on the trellis waiting for other birds, and it thrilled me to be out of town at last, especially with the promise of snow in the sky.

In front of me, the mountain
is covered with mist and, below me,
the lake is like a mirror.

Lough Allen was blue. The sky was blue
and cold. A long tuft of white cloud
   like cotton wool hung on the ridge of
Sliabh an Iarainn. Around me the alder
   trees and primroses were flourishing.
The slope of the lawn was riddled with
      holes where the badgers fed at night.
In the woods behind where I was sitting,
   there was a carpet of snowdrops.
A single magpie stood guard high up in
   a Scots pine. And along the beech hedge,
a wren was hopping about looking for
      things I knew nothing about.

And creeping buttercup everywhere,
tangled so densely through the long grass
that when drizzle fell a yellow hue
hung over the field. Whenever the
drizzle stopped, the clouds turned purple
and overhung the earth like the underbelly
of a gigantic fish touching the tip
of Sliabh an Iarainn and bringing an
astonishing intensity to the
yellow of the buttercup.

The trees hold me; their branches nurture me more effectively than the arms of a good mother. Sometimes they are like a cathedral of impermanence: in summer they burst with birdsong and in winter all the dead leaf rustles with hidden life beneath my feet. But only in autumn do they go silent, as if they were frightened of death.

In Donegal, the thread of a human life
    seems elegantly unimportant compared
to the sustained majesty of the earth lying
    all around like so much debris that
some giant had just abandoned.

The world is different at the seaside
or at the edge of an ocean.
There's a sense of permanence.
A sense of some presence beyond us,
which goes on for longer, and from
which we came and to which
we will some day return.

Falling snow is a chance to check
   out of life. To abandon the empty self,
to forget history, to leave aside every feud,
   wound, hurt or disgrace and begin again
to play like a child and construct a new
   identity with frozen fingers in the big
white wonder of a world made new.
      Snow meant time off to feed the birds
      and turn away.

The big snowflakes arrived.
Unexpected. *L*ike love letters.

Snow makes it easy to believe in
the invisible. And in the possibility of
    a human soul. A kind of deeper
hidden self, like a mountain
            obscured in a blizzard.

Over the years, the lawnmower became my ally. Its hum often made a blanket for my sorrow. The sound of it gave me something to hold on to, like a monk gripping his mantra with single-pointed attention. So, there I was on a quiet autumn afternoon, following a machine for two hours as it walked me around old memories.

This is the time when the trees around me and the grass beneath my feet feel like a mother's touch. I am awakening in my belonging as the morning breeze kisses my old face.

The Dysfunctional Elephant: thoughts on the Interior

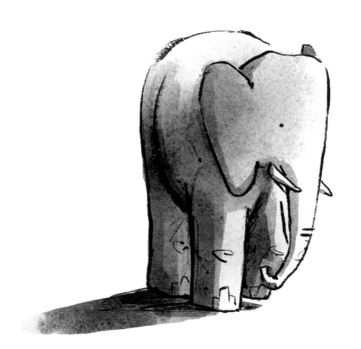

'The mind is like an elephant,' he said.
He would have heard the same phrase from
his own teachers when he was a young
student in some remote Tibetan monastery.
It's an image commonly used for the
unruly mind in lots of Tibetan texts on
mind training. The elephant goes
where it wants.

Sadness is not a bad thing, though lying in bed on a winter's day unable to do anything but weep is something most sensible people might try to avoid.

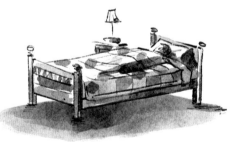

'I hear you ran into a bit of stormy weather,' someone said to me, after I had fallen apart. When I ended up in hospital and subsequently at home in bed, depressed for months. Stormy weather.
I suppose that's it all right.

Irish weather is the core of our melancholy,
    I thought. The unpredictability of it.
If it's raining, it's raining. If the sun is
    shining, the only question to ask is:
How long will it last? Not long. The fog
    comes again. Envelops us. No wonder
half the country is depressed.

It's only when I say 'I love you' that I know I love you. It's only when I say 'I am afraid' that I know I am afraid.

I went out one morning and sat on the old swing in the garden. I intended cutting the ropes and throwing the old plastic seat in the recycling, but there's something about an empty swing that is untouchable; and there's an absence in it, which nothing can cure. And that's where silence creeps in and stories die. Because it's too hard to talk about sorrow.

I told her that I had heard a poet declare
that there were three types of tears: the
tears that rise from grief, the tears
we shed when we don't get what we
want and the tears that never
come to the surface at all.

Nobody likes to talk about depression
in real life. It's only on the radio
that it sounds heroic.

It was like the tiredness that comes at the end of a party. When it's over. When you want to go home. Four-in-the-morning tiredness. When you have walked far enough and you want to lie down.

Tháinig uaigneas orm.

When you respect your darkest energy,
like anger, and when you are mindful
of it and when you hold and embrace it,
then you're less likely to be possessed
by it unconsciously. That's what I believe.

It was a miracle to be cheerful in _Leitrim_ during any winter. The county becomes a dark and bleak landscape of sitka trees and empty fields and old rusting sheds.

In winter, the cat would sometimes sit on the sill – inside, looking out – and I would say, 'Don't do that. Don't look out, you will only depress yourself.'

I am angry. It's a simple sentence.
But if I say it, and feel the truth of it,
then I feel better. In fact, I feel less angry
the more I become aware of how angry
I feel. If I can say, 'I'm angry,'
I know what is passing through me.

'Depression arrives like a flock of crows sometimes. But you must never let them sit,' the poet warned, and he dug his finger into my shoulder.

I spent all winter in the half-made house
    with a hole in the wall and a huge
empty hole in my gut, where God used
    to be. I sat by the fire for months and
nothing but sorrow came each evening
    with the encroaching dark.

What disturbed me most was the idea
that nothing would remain in my wake.
    Therefore, it was all meaningless.
It would all be forgotten.

It was like a mortal enemy had arrived.
It was the certainty that there are only
   so many days a human being can
remain standing.

I left her sleeping in the house and went back out into open air.

I was walking beautifully, slowly, barefoot, knowing that this was how to walk beautifully out of my anxieties. I saw the details of my life like little specks of snow falling not into me but away from me. Dropping down into an endless pit below me, a deep, white falling until I was just walking with no past or future.

I spoke nothing of how I felt to the beloved. Perhaps because there is an appropriate time for intimacy and an appropriate time for solitude. And my solitude had changed in her absence. It was no longer frightening or darkly lit, but more like a cloud where a bird rises and wings the wind and is delightfully alone.

What happens between one story and
the next? That's the really interesting part.
That's the space where we find bliss,
where we float sometimes, suspended,
and only for a brief moment.
Perhaps only for a few scarce
moments in an entire life.

My teacher used to tell me that the mind should be like a lake but not a river. It should be deep but not turbulent. And it should be as clear and bright as the sky in Mongolia, where things sparkle and where, in the empty blue, there are always beautiful things to be seen.

It was faint, but there was a sweet feeling of happiness in the twilight.

A voice inside me, akin to a wise man
   at the back of a cave, whispered,
'If you miss this moment,
      you will miss your life.'

The room was still dark but, through the window, I could see the sun's rays edging over the mountain.
The sky was clear.

Just to walk in snow was enough.

Listening to the Radio: thoughts on Togetherness

The wonderful thing about Ireland
is that, despite the Famine, the weather,
the clergy and the banks,
we still possess the brazen optimism to
engage with each other, to mind each
other and to hope for love around
the next corner.

It's in the story of the comings and goings, the ups and downs of ordinary folk to whom small things happen beautifully. That's where the miracles lie. That's the story that needs to be told over and over again.

Frisky boys who arrived on their tractors
on warm summer nights, fresh from
 mowing fields, their wheels leaving a trail
of grass on the dry roads. One driving
 while two others clung on, in standing
positions on the rear box, and the
     threesome smoking and looking as
magnificent as something from a
   Wagner opera as they arrived in the
car park for the dance.

In the olden days, men spent their time
   in the fields making hay and had no
feelings, and women were inside stirring
   pots of stew that later everyone ate at
the bare-board table on the flagstone floor
in a kind of monastic silence as they all
   inhabited the bliss of being a family.
That must have been really frightening.

The summer sky was always full of
   sound in _Leitrim_, from the booming bittern
to the cry of the curlew, but there was
   no sound as delicious as our neighbour's
tractor in a field nearby, as he sat steering
   and twisting his head to watch the rake
toss the mown grass into perfect lines
   behind him, and later the thump of hay
bales being piled into the red galvanised
   shed, where the cat moved in his wake
   as she hunted for field mice.

In the countryside, people who are isolated cannot bear to look at the blowing rain or hear the keening wind across all the bleak bogs and flooded fields.

So, they listen to the radio.

Single men with cupboards full of tablets listen. Unmarried brothers who once courted the same woman listen. Spinsters who live on sliced ham and wrinkled lettuce leaves from their own gardens listen.

Country people listen to the radio all day with a collective intensity that marks them out from city dwellers. They listen morning, noon and night. They stop what they're doing, they stand still with a dishtowel in the hand or they put down the razor or they become transfixed at the fire grate holding a coal scuttle just to hear the next sentence that the person on the wireless might utter.

'Did you hear that?' some man says, coming into the kitchen to address his wife, because there's always more than one radio in any house.

The details of funerals read out in solemn tones with soft music in the background to soothe the listeners, the women toiling at the sink in tears and the men at the dinner table with broken hearts.

We talk about nothing by talking about everything.

We were eating slices of pizza
   on the street. 'This is delicious,'
I said. My friend agreed.

Thus, we established a connection.
    Where are you from? And do I know
someone you know? And off we went
    over poached eggs and rashers and mugs
of tea, talking like two kings
          about the universe.

It's such a contentment to hold another
    human being, to abandon self-obsession,
leave personal anxieties forgotten in the
    past and reach forward towards other
beings. It's the kind of bliss that everyone
    talks about when they talk about being
in love. What the saints talked about when
they talked about a union with God,
    an awareness that, despite the atrocities of
life, you are always being held by someone.

Holding each other. Holding everything.
It's the ultimate reality.
Everything else is a delusion.

The assurance that you are held is
    something that grows stronger through
the years. It's all in the wonder of
    letting go and trusting to another.
It's the parachute jump without the
parachute. It's even a bit like faith in God,
    as we understood it in the old days,
    the sense of letting go completely and
trusting that the other person will hold you.

I went outside and phoned his old number.

I got an answering machine and his voice iterated a mobile number.

I phoned it. And suddenly, after all those years, we were connected,

just like that.

A stranger is always
the next great possibility.

Before the lockdowns she went to mass, received the host from a Eucharistic minister's hand, and sliced many scones to share with her best friend in a coffee shop on the way home. Even in Dunnes Stores, she used to bump against other people, and feel the touch of the young cashier's fingers as she paid for her groceries and the cashier passed the change back into her palm, counting the euros and the twenty-cent pieces, cent by tiny cent. A hairdresser would call to her house each week. It wasn't that she needed her hair perfectly shaped in silver-blue locks, but the accidental touch of the hairdresser's fingers kneading her scalp made a difference.

On my way home in silence.
More embraced. By her. By him.
By the woman at the boarding gate.
By the air steward. By the passengers.
By the world. Embraced. Entangled.
That was the feeling. That was good.

The writer rose to speak, an elderly man with white hair, and a soft but intense voice that contained the thunder of a life lived intensely and the controlled inflections of an experienced lover and performer. He stood for a moment in silence until he had gained attention. A pin dropping would have been noted.

'I remember being a child,' he began, 'and dreaming of two horses: a brown and a dove grey. It was my first dream, and now recently I see them again. They return in old age. Though not so much the brown, but more frequently the dove grey.'

In the modern world, this might have sounded obscure. Even at some poetry festival in the city, I could imagine people reaching for multiple references and instantly expecting a dissertation on psychoanalysis. But on the rugged faces of the unlettered people that packed into the parish hall in Bailieborough, who knew him since he was a child, and knew his mother and who saw him grow, bone of their bones, with nothing before him but the grave, his meaning was different.

One morning in a Galway hotel, I was in the sauna and the woman beside me was crying. I didn't know her. She was just another member of the leisure centre. But I had never seen anyone cry in the sauna before. The leisure centre was empty except for the two of us, so it didn't matter.

'I can barely get out of bed in the mornings,' she said. 'I don't know why.'

I didn't quite know what to say, but I tried as best I could to sound like a therapist. 'Perhaps you have lost interest in what is on the outside,' I said, 'because you are so unhappy on the inside.'

'Well, I think that's obvious,' she said, and she looked at me as if I was the worst therapist she had ever met, either in or out of a sauna. But at least she had stopped crying.

Only in the entanglement
with others can I be human.

When I first met the beloved I sang, 'Hold me close'. It was a song we hummed together in far-off countries, walking down unknown streets where other couples were leaning on balconies under blue skies.

And when I was away from her, in distant cities, I always ended up on a balcony on Sunday morning, looking out at the other apartment blocks around me and thinking to myself that the world was full of people holding each other. I would drink mint tea with lemon juice, and imagine them feeling happy and safe and sleepy, all in their private little apartments around me.

Sometimes, I say it when we are lying
in bed. I used to think it was risky.
   She might reject me, I thought.
One of these days, she might say,
   'No, I won't hold you any more. I'm fed
up holding you like you were some helpless
imbecile.' And then where would I be?
   I have said it on warm afternoons in
July. And in the kitchen after midnight
on Christmas Eve, when everyone had
   gone to bed. 'Hold me.' It's like a prayer.

When we were first married, we bought an enormous bed in Boyle that took up the entire bedroom of our small cottage in the hills, and though we could do very little else in that space, at least we were able to lie quietly on Sunday mornings holding each other for the entire length of 'Sunday Miscellany'.

I would lie there imagining people all over the world doing the same thing. Holding each other; in cities and remote villages, in apartment blocks, small cottages, under canvas roofs or straw roofs or under no roof at all.

And you don't actually have to say the words. Sometimes it's just a gesture. A woman on a Ryanair flight nudging closer to her husband, a man looking across the Formica table of a cheap restaurant at his partner as he seeks her approval before tucking into a large steak or a young girl dropping her head onto her boyfriend's shoulder on the bus to Cavan. They're all saying the same thing in their own way; they're all reaching out to hold each other.

Some years ago, there was a homeless couple who died in each other's arms as they slept in a doorway off Capel Street in Dublin. They were frozen to death in a cardboard box one frosty night. They hugged each other until the state pathologist parted them. Their intimacy was frozen stiff on an ice-covered street. The milkman found them the next day in the doorway, their bodies entwined by a mix of hunger, pain and love. They were old, alcoholic and homeless, and their minds too were probably twisted with psychic wounds and trans-generational traumas that never saw the light of day. But they held. They held each other tenderly as they fell into the silence of the night.

This Ordinary Place: thoughts on Philosophy

There was a time in west Cavan when people firmly believed in heaven. They would sing a hymn entitled 'Going Home' at the door of the church as the coffin was wheeled out into the wind on a trolley, along the uneven path of weeds and stones to the graveyard on the hill.

Old men at the cemetery gate would joke about what the theological implications might be if the coffin fell off the trolley. The sods clattered on the coffin lid. The diggers continued and people listened for the blade of the shovel hitting some stone or an ancestor's skull as the grave was finally closed in. But those sounds, of shovel in clay and stones on the coffin lid, clattering in the hole below our feet, called us beyond the pale moon of morning. The very sounds, or perhaps the silence between the sounds, implied something deeper in the still air — a sheltering place more true than death, and nobody was embarrassed to believe in it and call it heaven. The universe was limitless in its possibilities back then.

All I had to do was confess that I was in therapy or that I was depressed or confused about old age, and the room filled with advisors, confidants and people who used the word 'should' more than they should.

'You should try reiki. It's amazing.'

'You should go on holiday. Vitamin D is the answer.'

'You should garden.'

'You should read the book I sent you, it's about Freud.'

Cycle.

Lose weight.

Go to India.

Have a massage.

Talk to my friend.

Talk to my sister.

Try tai chi.

Eat avocados.

Meditate.

I tried everything. All those and more. Sometimes the country seemed to be swarming with evangelical therapists!

I get lyrical in the mornings.
I cannot resist the glory of heaven in
this ordinary place. And I am here.
I am present. And today is the day
we had been waiting for.

A story is the most beautiful way of
bearing witness to the world.
Even lovers are more present to each other
   when they speak their stories in whispers
on the pillow or casually confess their
   private histories as they busy themselves
in the kitchen, caught up in the mundane
   entanglement of cooking food.

If you think you're meditating, then maybe
    you're not. If you think you're not, then
maybe you are. As they say in Japan,
    'If you name the bird, then you cease to
experience the song.' So, in naming the
    act of meditation you cease to meditate.
Personally, I just doze. I think dozing
    might be described as the
        Irish tradition of meditation.

Doing nothing is still doing something. So, the wisdom is in the not doing. The complete non-involvement in anything. Stillness. And if that's not a sure way to induce a beautiful doze, then nothing is.

Everyone wonders. Everyone asks,
'What have I done?' Maybe that's the
question that makes us human.

In childhood, we were always waiting for something. We all waited as we sat around in pubs or near the open fire or in fields of summer. I used to think it was the essence of being Irish, to wait and doze by the fire. Waiting for friends, for letters, for the nine o'clock news, for exam results, the visa in the post, the mother to die, the mass to be over. There was a great patience in people back then. They waited.

When nothing happens for the entire afternoon, it's lovely to just feel you are there. To be aware that you are there. It's what I used to be accused of doing in school. Back then, it was called daydreaming. But, today, as I pay attention to the flame in the stove, the flickering shadow or the movement of a bird on a tree outside or the tiny shifting of the curtains with the wind, I am not dreaming. I am awake in my lovely dozing. I feel like a baby in a cot with open eyes. I know I'm there. And I feel like an old man by the fire who knows that he has only a short while to live and that the clock is ticking and each moment is precious.

But there is a deeper waiting, I thought,
   as I walked around Warsaw in the snow,
making my way between the tall black trees,
   up the hill towards the statue of Charles
de Gaulle and then around by the Church
of the Three Crosses and back down
   through the woods again. I had come to
Poland for nothing. I had no reason to
   be there. I had no cause to pursue or goal
to attain in Warsaw. I was just waiting.
   Waiting for nothing.

Maybe enlightenment is nothing
more than a highly developed emotional
intelligence, what used to be described
as common sense — a word that long ago
faded from the lexicon of mental health.

I know that there are no ghosts in the
modern world — I suppose it may have been
electric light that finished them off —
but maybe there are angels.

Some people come into our lives like
guardians from other worlds. It is as if
they were sent to watch over us,
to give us some indefinable
sustenance on our journey.

I couldn't tell anyone that I believed in angels or that sometimes in winter as the snow fell, I would feel myself blessed as I walked through it, shaking the white tufts from my boot.

Music teaches a simple lesson.
  Wait for the tune. Play the tune.
Be present in every moment.
  That seemed clearer than anything
I ever found in the libraries of
  religion or philosophy.

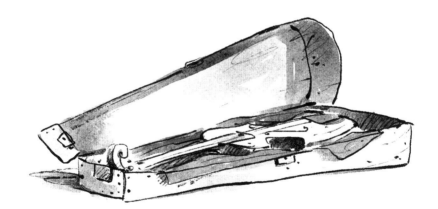

I imagined heaven as
an act of love and faith
in the absurdity of eternal life.

I long for heaven in the face of death.
I long for heaven because although
there is no heaven, it does me good
just to long for it.

'The mind is like the sky,' my teacher
    would say, 'and your actions should be
like eagles that hover very high over the
    world. The eagle only occasionally flaps
its wings to retain height, and your
    actions should never be like the
        sparrow that does a lot of flapping
but never achieves altitude.'

Prayer is a secret activity.
It's a private adventure, a journey
to the heart's core.

'Every man must walk over a cliff.'
I presumed he meant it in the sense of
    taking risks. 'Oh you're right there,'
says I. 'Blindfolded,' he added.
        'A man must walk over the cliff
blindfolded!' He was animated.
        The wind around his head.
'And regularly!' he roared.

One day, I was sitting at the back of the classroom on an Irish-language summer course in Donegal with a grammar book on the desk when a new student slipped into the seat beside me. A strong-featured man with hair turning grey and the curiosity of an eagle.

'A Mhichíl,' he said, 'is it yourself, by God?'

(That's just a translation.)

'It is me surely, by God,' I replied.

We didn't speak in English, so our conversation was limited. At the coffee break, we shared a plate of gingernut biscuits and chatted about the upcoming Armagh-Donegal match.

'Is it yourself will be looking at the match?' I wondered.

'No,' he replied, 'I am not looking at it. But perhaps I might be in it.'

That sounded like he was on the team, and I could see why Armagh was the underdog if they were fielding players in their mid-fifties.

'Accept my apology,' he said. 'Accept my thousand sorrows. What is being said with me is that I am going to the game. I will be looking at the match from the stage.'

He meant the stand, but we had so few words.

And thus we talked our pidgin Irish each morning, like shell-shocked veterans of our long lives and our own private catastrophes, because we were stuck with the limited phrases of our college days when we were both studying for the priesthood. He'd left before ordination, and I'd stayed in for a few short years, knowing that, in the end, there was no place in the Church for me.

There was a lot we could have spoken of, if we'd been speaking English or if we'd been fluent in the native Irish tongue. We could have gossiped a bit and expressed shock at the state of the world. Or we might just have spoken of the women in our own lives, and how they had shifted our perspective over the years and of how naive we had been back then.

But we discussed none of these things.

'The day is good.'

'The day is bad!'
'The day is amazing!'
(Lá maith. Droch lá. Lá iontach.)
    And eventually, like a haiku, the changing sky became a metaphor for how we felt, and the weather outside the window carried our emotions. We narrowed ourselves into small phrases. We bent the empirical world to our own capacity for expression.
    'Lá breá' began to mean everything.
    We had fallen by accident into a state of zen. We were alive and human, sitting in each moment like magpies on an ash tree.

When the Irish language course was over, I packed my bag and cleared out of the house where I had been staying. I packed my notebooks and the grammar book the teacher had been referring us to all week. But I knew I would never use it again. Flipping through the pages of Cruinnscríobh na Gaeilge, felt like a lost life. All those verbs and nouns and other beautiful words would never be mine. It was too late. The Gaelic language I had tried to learn as a child was gone from me forever. But at least the course had taught me that through simple sentences, the mind can remain very much in the present moment.

And instead of being uneasy that the beloved and I sometimes said very little to each other, I realised as I drove home that we had, over the years and in our own inarticulate blundering, been practising a language of love.